Noff's Hot Dogs
Guide to Success

Noff's Hot Dogs Guide to Success

James Mazzola

To order additional copies of this book, contact:
Xlibris Corporation
1-888-795-4274
www.Xlibris.com
Orders@Xlibris.com
65398

CONTENTS

WELCOME TO NOFF'S HOT DOGS!

Thank you for your interest in joining our growing family of Noff's Hot Dogs and for giving us the opportunity to help you succeed in your new business. With Noff's you will enjoy the feeling of owning your own business, ongoing training, and the community of Noff's owner-operators who share your enthusiasm. Best of all, you will have fun building your own business—and you won't be doing it alone.

Whether you are making a career change, exploring ways to increase your income, or seeing what it is like to have your own business for the first time, I believe Noff's can help you realize your goals and potential. With the extra income you earn, you will be able to meet more of your financial needs—and do some of the "extra" activities you have been dreaming about.

You are also going to have a great time meeting new people, learning new skills, and building on your own talents. I say that with complete confidence because that is what happened to me when I took over my family's business.

Noff's Hot Dogs was established in 1919. Antonio Mazzola, an Italian immigrant, came from Sorrento to the city of Hoboken, New Jersey, where he opened his first cart, serving both the rich and the poor with relish and respect. My mission is to create an opportunity for anyone with the interest, desire, and commitment to take advantage of the opportunities the United States has to offer, regardless of technical experience, and to build a home-based business that is personally and financially rewarding.

So welcome to Noff's Hot Dogs and its opportunity to improve your life in unexpected ways, an opportunity to "find value" for yourself and for a world of people who are going to be happy about your new venture—and the valuable service you can offer them.

I wish you outstanding success!

James Mazzola

MY VALUES AND PRINCIPLES

My values

- Respect
  Treat others as you want to be treated
- Quality
  Provide a service that is outstanding in its value and courtesy
- Opportunity
  Create an opportunity that enables people to reach their full potential and earn at their personal level of time and commitment
- Community
  Encourage the spirit of teamwork and foster learning through knowledge and communication
- Innovation
  Celebrate the positive values and innovative spirit of Noff's Hot Dogs

My principles

- Satisfy customers' needs while surpassing their expectations.
- Serve each customer as though it was his or her first time.
- Uphold the highest professional standards of integrity, honesty, and responsibility.

INTRODUCTION

You might think it is hard to start a hot dog cart business. To get you started on your way, I have compiled everything you need in one comprehensive manual.

This manual is designed to provide you with all the information you will need to establish, run, and grow your hot dog business. It will help you decide what type of hot dog business you want to run. Do you want to work full-time or part-time, permanent or temporary locations? This manual will show you what you need to run your hot dog business.

I have also included proven condiment recipes, inventory control, accounting, and even tips on how to deal with your customers.

It is my hope that after you read this manual, you will follow it step-by-step; and in a few short months, you will be running you own hot dog business

WHAT IS A HOT DOG?

From Wikipedia, the free encyclopedia

A hot dog (frankfurter, frank, wiener, weenie, dog) is a moist sausage of soft, even texture and flavor, often made from mechanically recovered meat or meat slurry. Most types are fully cooked, cured, or smoked. It is often placed hot in a special-purpose, soft, sliced hot dog bun. It may be garnished with mustard, ketchup, onion, sauerkraut, relish, cheese, or chili. The flavor can be similar to a range of meat products from bland bologna to spicy German bratwurst varieties. Kosher hot dogs may be made from beef, chicken, or turkey. Vegetarian hot dogs made from meat analogue are available.

Unlike other sausages, which may be sold uncooked, hot dogs are always cooked. Unless spoiled, hot dogs can be eaten without cooking, although they are usually warmed before serving.

HISTORY OF THE HOT DOG

Also called frankfurters, franks, weenies, wieners, dogs, and red hots, they consist of a combination or either beef and pork or all beef, which is cured, smoked, and cooked. Seasonings may include coriander, garlic, ground mustard, nutmeg, salt, sugar, and white pepper. They are fully cooked but are usually served hot. Sizes range from big dinner frankfuters to tiny cocktail size.

No one will ever know who invented the sausage, but one of the oldest forms of processed food is mentioned in Homer's *Odyssey* in the ninth century BC. Other references go back further to 1500 BC in Babylon.

In AD 64, Emperor Nero Claudius Caesar's cook, Gaius, is often credited with discovering the first sausage. According to a legend, a pig was roasted. But for some reason, it was not cleaned and gutted. When Gaius cut into the pig's belly, to his surprise, out popped the intestines, and they were puffed and hollow. Gaius then stuffed the intestines with a ground beef mixture and some spices and tied the ends, thus creating the first wiener.

However, a Frankfurt man in Germany is usually credited with the origination of the frankfurter in 1484, five years before Christopher Columbus set sail for the New World. In the 1850s, the Germans made thick, soft, and fatty sausages from which we get the famed "franks."

German immigrants appear to have sold hot dogs, along with milk, rolls and sauerkraut, from pushcarts in New York City during the 1860s. Charles Feltman, a German butcher, is said to have been the first vendor when he opened his pie wagon in Coney Island.

In 1893 in Chicago, the Columbian Exposition brought hordes of visitors who consumed large quantities of sausages sold by vendors. People liked this food because it was easy to eat, convenient, and inexpensive. That same year, sausages became standard at ballparks. A St. Louis bar owner, Chris Von de Ahe, who owned the St. Louis Browns major league baseball team, began this tradition.

The earliest usage of hot dog in clear reference to sausage was found in the September 28, 1893, edition of *The Knoxville Journal* in the article "The Sic Wove Overcoats," page 5.

> It was so cool last night the appearance of overcoats was common, and stoves and grates were again brought into comfortable use. Even the weinerwurst men began preparing to get the hot dogs ready for sale Saturday night.

In 1894, sausage vendors would sell their wares outside the student dorms and major eastern universities, and their carts became known as "dog wagons." The name was a sarcastic comment on the source of the meat. The slang term came from the popular belief that dog meat was used in making sausage.

Another early use of the complete phrase "hot dog" in reference to sausage appeared on page 4 of the October 19, 1895, issue of *The Yale Record*: "They contentedly munched hot dogs during the whole service."

The term hot dog was coined in 1901 at the New York Polo Grounds. On a cold April day, concessionaire Harry Stevens was losing money on ice cream and cold soda. He sent venders to buy up all the dachshund sausages they could find and an equal number of rolls. In less than an hour these vendors were hawking the dogs from portable hot water tanks. In the press box, sports cartoonist Tad Dorgan, not sure how to spell the word "dachshund," simply wrote "*hot dog!*" The cartoon was a sensation; the term hot dog was born, and the rest is history.

STARTING A BUSINESS

When starting a new business, there are many important decisions to make and many rules and procedures that must be addressed. While there is no single source for every state, the following steps have been developed to assist you in starting your business.

Select a Name and Legal Structure

Your name is something you can choose for any reason. You basically have four choices when selecting a legal structure:

1. Sole proprietorship
2. Partnership
3. Limited liability corporation
4. Corporation

Sole Proprietorship in general can be established with little or no formalities. However, it will generally be necessary to obtain one or more local business licenses from the cities and or counties in which you will operate, and in some cases, you might need a state license as well. If you make sales of tangible property at a retail level, you will be required to obtain a sales tax license for the collecting of sales tax.

No separate tax-form filing is required. You simply report that your business financial information on standard tax forms is available for sole proprietorships.

Doing business as a sole proprietor is much simpler than operating as any other kind of business legal entity. If you have no employees, you are not required to pay or withhold any unemployment taxes, withhold any federal or state income tax from wages, or obtain workers' compensation coverage for yourself.

Partnerships allow the creation of either a general partnership in which all partners are liable for the debts of the business, or a limited partnership, in which only the general partners are liable for debts. It is generally necessary to obtain one or more local business licenses from the cities, counties, and possibly the state in which you will operate.

Partnerships, as entities, are not subject to state income tax. Instead, the income or loss of the partnership, as allocated among the partners, must be reported on the personal income tax returns of each individual partner. However, there might be some local or state annual fees or tax required.

A partnership agreement, for any type of partnership, should spell out in considerable detail all aspects of the partnership. It is recommended that you contact both an attorney and an accountant to discuss all the legal and financial aspects of your partnership agreement and make sure it is all in writing.

Concerning *corporations*, a business may incorporate without an attorney, but legal advice is highly recommended. The corporate structure is usually complex and more costly to organize. Control depends on stock ownership. Persons with the largest stock ownership control the corporation. All corporations must file articles of incorporation with the business services office in the state you wish to operate in.

Limited liability companies (LLC) are very attractive entities for many small businesses. While offering much of the flexibility plus the flow through tax treatment of a partnership for federal and state income tax purposes, there might be fees and permits required for city, county, and state levels.

With both options, it is recommended that you contact both an attorney and an accountant to discuss all the legal and financial aspects of corporation and LLC.

For someone who is just starting out, you might want to be a sole proprietor. This is the easiest and least expensive option to get started with. As your business grows and you hire employees or expand your operation, you should discuss the other options with an attorney and your accountant.

Taxation

All businesses must pay taxes. When you register your business, most states and the federal government will require pertinent forms for compliance. A business start date is very important because you will be required to file income taxes and collect sales tax from that day.

Open a Company Bank Account

Once you have established your business name, formed your legal structure, and taken care of all legal tasks, you have to open a bank account for your business. One simple business checking account should be fine. As your business grows, you can discuss other options with your accountant.

Insurance

You should have the proper insurance for all of your equipment and vehicles as required by law or needed. Some jurisdictions may require you to carry business liability insurance. This can be obtained for around $200 to $500 per year.

HOT DOG VENDING

- Be your own boss
- Low start-up costs
- Set your own hours
- Work the big events—fairs, parades, and special events
- Work a dedicated location
- Rent your cart for promotional events
- All-cash business
- Every day is payday
- Hot dog vending requires little or no overhead
- The average cost of a hot dog is $0.60
- Most vendors sell hot dogs for $1.25-$2.50
- Most vendors sell hot dogs five days a week
- Work part-time to supplement your income
- If you sold one hundred hot dogs per day, you would make over $35,000 per year
- If you sold two hundred and fifty hot dogs per day, you would make over $80,000 per year
- Over one thousand hot dogs are eaten every second of every day of every year
- An average person eats fifty hot dogs every year

Though no single food-service operation has universal appeal, almost everyone loves hot dogs. With over 350 million men, women, and children in America, hot dogs provide a high-quality, low-cost meal.

Hot dog sales are up. Consumers are trading down rather than going to casual dining establishments. Hot dog stands are capitalizing on these food trends. They are cheap; the food is fresh, customizable, and portable; and if properly made, they taste really good.

Disposable income is not a factor. In good times, people eat fast. In bad times, people eat cheap. But they have to eat.

No one knows how many hot dogs are served daily. But because of their size and texture, hot dogs are one of the most common finger foods given to children. As the population increases and becomes more mobile, these estimates are anticipated to increase.

Industry Analysis

The retail hot dog industry consists of mom-and-pop owner-operators. The quality and consistency of these hot dogs varies greatly. Franchises account for no significant market presence. Even though 7-Eleven is North America's number-one retailer of fresh, grilled hot dogs, the hot dogs that are sold in convenience stores and gas station are generally low grade and of poor quality.

Industry Participants

There are only about a dozen hot dog franchises. There are only three who have more than one hundred units, and none of them have more the four hundred. Nathan's Famous, Wienerschnitzel, and Woody's Chicago Style have limited, local-market presence only. These are generally regional and have no national-name recognition. Other chains also sell them, which includes Sonic Drive-In, Hardee's, and Dairy Queen; but since they gear to fixed-store locations, a more diverse menu, and the initial start-up cost, this puts it out of reach of most franchisers and operators. Casual dining restaurants often have hot dogs on their children's menu, but not on the regular menu; however, other mom-and-pop operators pose the only significant competition.

Local Competition

There are really no national chains that pose much competition. Convenience stores and gas stations generally provide low-grade, poor-quality hot dogs. And since most mom-and-pop operators only serve a very small geographical area, they are only known in a few mile radius of their location.

You may be surprised by how simple it is to get a hot dog stand started. Here is a step-by-step manual to start, operate, and grow your business:

Step 1

Develop a Selling Strategy

The first thing you need is to determine where you want to sell hot dogs. You basically have a few choices. You can find a permanent location or you can work events such as fairs, carnivals, parades, etc. There are advantages to both cases. Working events gives you the ability to earn lots of money in a relatively short period of time. This is an ideal approach for someone interested in doing this part-time. If you choose this option, please keep records on when these events are. You might have to register and/or pay for the location in advance of the event.

If you opt for selecting a permanent location, there is no magic way to pick out a good spot. You are seeking an area with either high foot traffic or a large volume of commuter traffic passing by. Commuters are defined as anyone or more individuals traveling from point A to point B. If you decide to sell at the roadside, be sure you select a spot where there is room for your customers to safely park. You should look for an area where there are no other food-serving establishments nearby. The greatest concentration will be on the commuters heading to and from work or school, or those out on their lunch break. There are exceptions to this rule. For example, in a busy downtown area, you could have hot dog vendors on every corner, and they could still all make a nice living.

Some vendors opt to locate on private property where there are captive consumers. These are defined as those who are "tethered" to a campus or those that are in a restricted environment that does not allow free movement to and from. Parking lots of large malls or stores where there is little or no food being served can be quite lucrative. College campuses, businesses without a cafeteria, etc., can be goldmines. Special events—such as carnivals, fairs, festivals, or concerts—where admission prices can be done on a part-time basis. If you decide to do this, there will likely be a lease expense to the owner of the building or area for the right to locate on their property.

Permanent Locations

1. Busy street corner
2. Roadsides
3. Large home stores (Home Depot, Lowe's, etc.)
4. Large automotive chain stores
5. Beaches
6. Parks
7. Strip malls
8. Industrial parks
9. Government complexes
10. Factories
11. Military bases
12. Amusements parks, boardwalks
13. Waste disposal centers, quarries, mines
14. Parking lots
15. Golf courses
16. Schools (high schools, colleges, universities)
17. Hospitals
18. Sports fields

Special Events and Temporary Locations

1. Sporting events
2. Carnivals
3. Street fairs and parades
4. Large construction sites
5. Conventions
6. Car shows and rallies
7. Festivals and shows
8. Contests and auctions

9. Charity, church, local, and government functions
10. Grand openings and dedications
11. Private parties
12. Corporate functions
13. Beaches, zoos, marinas, and tourist attractions
14. Flea markets and swap meets
15. Theaters and stadiums

Seasonal Locations

1. Beaches, piers, and marinas
2. Zoos and parks
3. Tourist attractions
4. Ski slopes

Catering

1. Private parties (birthdays, school parties, anniversaries, and theme parties)
2. Company and business events and picnics

Step 2

Select Your Vending Cart

When selecting your vending cart, you should look for the following features:

1. Mobility
2. Functionality
3. Ability to handle large volume
4. Cost
5. Locating/finding a cart

Mobility

In most cases, even if you have a permanent spot, you will need to transport your cart from your place of business or your home to the spot where you will sell. For this reason, it is imperative to have a cart that is easy to transport. Even if you have a situation where you can leave your cart in the same spot without moving it at all, you still should consider a mobile cart. It is best to be flexible.

Functionality

If you want to sell hot dogs, then you need a cart that can perform that function efficiently. Look for a unit that can be used immediately upon delivery. Look for a unit that you can roll off the truck and be in business on the same day.

I recommend a four-pot cooking area with two separate burners. These pots should consist of two half-sized hanging pots and two quarter-sized hanging pots either six or eight inches deep. They must be side-hinged. If you are buying a hot dog cart, be sure to have a ledge on each side with a lip bent up to avoid your products from falling off the cart. If you have a trailer, be sure to have a large enough serving counter so you and your customers can handle the food easily.

If a four-pot cooking area is not available, then you can work with a three-pot system. These generally will only have one burner. If you are not doing a very large volume, this option will be fine. You should have one half-sized pot and two quarter—sized hanging pots at least six to eight inches deep with side hinges.

With either system, you will need up to six condiment pots depending on your needs and what you want to serve. These pots sink in the water to heat your condiments.

Ability to Handle Large Volume

There would be nothing worse than finding a great spot, doing a great business, and then finding that your cart cannot handle the volume. Be sure to purchase a cart that can handle greater volume than you anticipate.

Either a three-or four-pot system will have the ability to serve up to six hot or warm condiments. As you become more experienced and developed a routine, you should be able to serve your hot dogs fast enough to manage your growing business. When the time comes and you need to or want to grow your business, you will have the knowledge the make a decision on the new equipment needed for your expansion plans.

Cost

Carts and trailers range from $500 for a used one up to $50,000 plus for some of the most expensive models with all the bells and whistles. I will not tell you that a buck is a buck. I will not recommend that you cut corners when purchasing your cart either. You will have it for a long time. However, do not get a cart that has more bells and whistles than you require. That would be a waste of good money. It is a good idea to buy a cart to fit your needs today as well as for your business's future growth.

Location/Finding a Cart

Once you have decided on which type of business you want to run, you must now find your cart or trailer. The first thing you should do is talk to someone who is doing the same type of business you want to operate. Hot dog vendors are generally very friendly. It is part of our nature. So most of us will help you by explaining how the business works and where you can find a cart.

Once you have decided on what type of hot dog cart you want, there are several options available. Do you want to purchase a new or used one?

If you decide to purchase a new one, you can find several hot dog cart manufactures in the Yellow Pages or on the Internet. When negotiating a price, please remember the shipping cost. The farther you look from where you want to operate, the more your shipping costs will be. Also, find out how fast they can ship inventory to you when your equipment needs replacements parts.

If you want to purchase a used hot dog cart, you might want to again ask your local hot dog vendor if they know anyone selling one. This is the business they are in. They speak to other hot dog vendors all the time. I would not be surprised if they refer you to someone they know who has one for sale.

You can also check the classified section of your local newspaper or Internet sites.

Two of the best sites are *www.ebay.com* and *www.craigslist.com*. You might want to look at hot dog carts close to you because most of the time, you will be responsible for any transportation costs.

Whether you buy a new or used hot dog cart, a high-quality one will last a very long time. I have one that was made in 1957. I consider them very large stainless steel pots. If you take care of them, they can last for decades.

Funding Your Business

How much money do you need? Your biggest expense will be your initial equipment. Regardless of how much you need, you might need additional funding to start your business. Here are some suggestions for start-up funds:

- *Your own resources.* Do a thorough inventory of you assets. People generally have more assets than they realize, including saving accounts, retirement accounts, equity in real estate, vehicles, collections, and other investments. You might opt to sell some of these assets, cash them in, or use them for collateral for a loan. Many successful businesses were started using credit cards.
- *Family and friends.* The next step after examining your resources is to approach family and friends who believe in you.
- *Partners.* Using the strength-in-numbers principle, you might want approach individuals who can afford to take a risk in investing in your business.

- *Government programs.* You might want to try and take advantage of local, state, and federal programs available to help small businesses. Make sure your first stop is the SPA. Women, minorities, and veterans should check out special financing programs designed to help them.
- *Vendor financing.* Many vendors offer financing or low-cost, rent-to-own programs.

Step 3

Calculate Your Budget

Your biggest expense for getting started will be the hot dog cart itself; however, there are a few more expenses to consider:

- State, federal and county costs
- Health and fire inspections costs
- Permit/license costs
- Zoning requirements
- Commissary expenses
- Registration expenses
- Lease expenses
- Initial inventory
- Storage costs
- Finance or loan payments
- Insurance
- Monthly fees
- Power supply

Some of these expenses may not apply in your situation.

State, Federal, and County Government Costs

You have to register your business name with all of the local government agencies that are required for your location as well as the federal government. You also have to obtain the proper sales tax information. If you incorporate, there are other legal costs involved.

Health Inspection Costs

Generally, there will be a charge for the health inspector to look at your cart. These costs vary widely from place to place. You can expect anywhere from $25 to $250. Contact your local health department to determine what the expenses will be.

Permit/License Costs

The type of permit/license you will need varies widely from place to place. The cost of these permits/licenses also varies widely. Contact your local health department to determine what these expenses will be. You might also need to have a criminal background check. Please contact the city officials in your area for local guidelines.

Zoning Requirements

Check with the local zoning office to determine if your business is in compliance with local zoning ordinances. If not, you might have to pay to make it conform to local zoning requirements or pay legal fees to have it complied.

Commissary Expenses

Some jurisdictions require you to operate from a licensed food establishment. All of your food must be delivered and stored there and various cleaning facilities must be available to you to clean your cart and utensils, and dispose of garbage, etc.

Registration Expenses

Many states will require you to obtain a license plate for your trailer or cart. If this is the case, contact you local department of motor vehicles to determine what the cost will be.

Lease Expense

If you decide to locate on private property, there may be a lease fee you will have to pay the property owner.

Initial Inventory

You can start your hot dog business very comfortably with $300 to $500 of inventory.

Storage

If you do not have enough room to store you cart at you home, you might have to rent a storage location. All you will need is a place to store your cart securely.

Finance or Loan Payments

You might also have finance or loan payments if you chose to take out a loan for the enrollment fee and hot dog cart purchase.

Insurance

You might have insurance costs depending on local and equipment requirements.

Power Supply

If you have a fixed location, you might have to pay to install electrical outlets. You might also have to pay for local inspections. If you are a mobile unit, you might have to purchase a fuel-powered generator.

Step 4

Meet with the Health and Fire Inspectors

At this point you will not have your cart; however, you should have sufficient information in hand that shows the design of the cart you are planning to purchase. Take this package to the health inspector and allow him or her to review it. He or she should know if the cart meets health department requirements. Most new carts meet health department requirements, but some jurisdictions have their own idiosyncrasies and may have some unique requirements. If the health inspector informs you the cart looks OK, then you should be fine.

Possible Requirements

What type of cooking system is allowed?

1. Gas
2. Propane
3. Electric
4. Grill

Do they allow pushcarts or enclosed trailers?
Do you need sinks and/or running water?
Do you need a refrigerator or freezer, or will coolers be OK?

Trailers might have more requirements:

1. Serving windows
2. Running water with waste collection
3. Screens
4. Vents
5. Hoods
6. Hot plate or microwave

You might need a fire inspection and will be required to purchase and maintain a fire extinguisher.

Contact List

Vending License or Permit Contact
Name: _____
Phone: _____
Fee: _____

Health Inspector
Name: _____
Phone: _____
Fee: _____

Zoning Officer
Name: _____
Phone: _____
Fee: _____

Fire Department
Name: _____
Phone: _____
Fee: _____

Insurance Company
Name: _____
Phone: _____
Fee: _____

Commissary
Name: _____
Phone: _____

Step 5

Put It Down on Paper

This is where the rubber starts to meet the road. Listed below are the required items you will need to start your business:

1. Hot dogs
2. Hot dog rolls
3. Sauerkraut
4. Chili
5. Onion sauce
6. Mustard
7. Ketchup
8. Relish
9. Cheddar cheese
10. Citrus heaven (orange and lemonade)
11. Private-label soda (optional)

Other products are required, but can be varied to the owner operator's individual requirements:

1. Chili (a proven recipe will be provided)
2. Onions (a proven recipe will be provided)
3. Name-brand soda and other beverages (water, iced tea, lemonade, Yoo-hoo, sports drinks, health drinks)
4. Napkins, bags, straws, cups and lids, take-out containers
5. You might require other products depending on your customers' requirements or tastes.

Note: You may take the start-up easy. Instead of buying everything in bulk at the onset, it may be wiser to start out easy and simply buy as you need or only a week in advance. Once you become established, you will know what inventory is required and how to manage it.

Some people might find it easier to have all of the supplies and inventory purchased and delivered buy one or two providers. The cost might be a little more expensive, but the convenience might make it worth your time.

Treat your vendors, manufacturers, and service providers with respect and let them know you appreciate them. They are an important part of your business success. If you talk down to them, pester them, imply that they do not do a good job, nickel-and-dime them to death, or are just a pain in the neck, they'll never go out of their way to help you. They might drop you all together. No business needs a picky, annoying, time-consuming customer. Simple courtesy and appreciation can go a long way to your growth.

Supplies

If you are located in the Northeast, I recommend the following suppliers:

Somerset Syrup
100 McGraw Drive
Edison, NJ 08837

Pirylis Distributors
221 Sussex Avenue
Newark, NJ, 07103

Restaurant Depot
www.restaurantdepot.com

For all other locations, you should ask a local hot dog vendor, the person who sold you his or her hot dog cart, or the dealer who is selling you a new hot dog cart. They will know the local inventory suppliers who can serve you best. You might also visit the major big-box wholesale stores such as the following:

- Sam's Club
- Costco
- Price Club
- BJ's Wholesale Club

All of these stores have special service hours for small business owners like you.

Step 6

Order Your Hot Dog Cart

At this point, the research has been done. Based on your requirements, it is time to order your new cart.

Step 7

Obtain Permits, Licenses, and Inspections

Some of the licenses can be obtained before your cart arrives. Make sure you get them in advance if you can. For those items that must wait until you have your cart in possession, get them done immediately upon receiving your cart. If you have done your homework, this step should proceed smoothly.

Start-up Worksheet

Legal Costs
1. Business license fee $_____
2. Health inspection fee $_____
3. Criminal background check $_____
4. Vendor license fee $_____

Start-up Costs
1. Cart and equipment purchase $_____
2. First month's rent $_____
3. Business insurance $_____
4. Franchise fee $_____

Operation Fees
1. Initial inventory food and supplies $_____
2. Cart storage $_____
3. Rent or location fees $_____
4. Business supplies and expenses $_____

Other
1. Food-handler training cost $_____
2. Advertising $_____
3. Other $_____

Total $_____

Step 8

Sell, Sell, Sell

Well, the day has arrived. Get up early, get organized, and get to your spot, then sell, sell, sell. Just remember one thing: a little courtesy and kindness go a long way in this hustle-bustle world. If your customers think you are a nice guy or a nice woman, they will come back. This is the idea instilled by my father Onofrio "Noff" Mazzola:

> At his hot dog wagon, when a child came up and asked for a hot dog, and the child only had a nickel, a nickel was enough. When a needy person would ask him for a free hot dog, Noff never turned them away. Even if that same person came back day after day.

> That child became an adult and will be your customer for life. Plus he or she will bring his or her children and friends, thus building a tradition that can last a lifetime.

Give it time. It takes a while to develop a real business. The key is to be consistent. Customers have to know what to expect. They want to expect the same quality of food and the knowledge of your hours of operation. Once the customers know this, your business is on its way.

As time goes on, you will learn to prepare yourself to handle your daily volume. The busy times are from seven thirty to nine o'clock, which is generally the breakfast and commuter crowd. Then you will be slow until about ten forty-five; this starts your lunch crowd, which lasts until about one thirty. From two thirty to four o'clock is a late-afternoon and after-school snack. Depending on the weather and daylight, a dinner rush will start from four forty-five until six o'clock. Roadside and campus locations might be different depending on road traffic, class schedules, and work breaks. The more of these peak eating-times you work, the more money you will make.

Note: Please be aware of seasonal changes and bad weather. Hot summer days are great at the beach, but not as profitable in urban areas. Cold, rain, and snowy days might cause additional problems. As your business progresses, you will be able to manage these temporary changes as they occur.

Step 9

Add Extra Items

For the first few weeks, do not fool around. Concentrate on selling your staples: hot dogs, soda, and chips. Once you get comfortable with these, try a few different items. Keep the winners and eliminate the nonprofitable items, but keep trying new items.

Seasonable items are very profitable

1. Green hats and buttons for St. Patrick's Day
2. Flags and banners for the Fourth of July
3. Baseball caps of local sporting events or teams

Step 10

Do Not Get Complacent

Do not treat your customers poorly; always be friendly, no matter how bad of a day you are having. Consistently analyze your situation. Keep experimenting; keep trying new food and other items.

TIME TO GET STARTED!

You are about to embark on the most exciting part of your new hot dog business—learning how to run your business and becoming a huge success. Our proven methods, products, recipes, knowledge, and skill will provide you with the skills and expertise necessary to get your business off to a solid start.

With over ninety years of family experience, my approach consists of the following criteria:

- Consistency—to be successful, you have to be consistent. You have to provide the same quality every time. Customers' expectations should be met or exceeded. Remember, you only have one time to make a first impression.
- Consistency—to be successful, you have to have consistent hours. Though you might only want to do the business part-time, you have to be consistent. If you only want to work weekends, then you have to be there every weekend. Your customers will come to expect you to be there. If you are not there, then they will go elsewhere.
- Consistency—to be successful, you have to be consistently nice. You will find that the same customers will come time and time again. Treat them nice, and they will come forever and also tell everyone they know. A referral is the best form of advertising.

Note: This is your own business. Treat the customers the same way you want to be treated.

WHAT YOU NEED TO OPERATE

The Basics

The following are the mandatory items you will need to get started. I will also offer tips for both short—and long-term operations.

Keep a binder or folder in your cart or vehicle that includes the following information:

1. Business or vendor license
2. Location license or rental agreement
3. Health license or permit
4. Temporary license or permit
5. Fire inspection and extinguisher, if required

Hot Dogs

You cannot run a hot dog cart without selling hot dogs. There are two types as the following:

Natural-casing hot dogs must be in the casing to be cooked. Traditionally, this casing is made from the thoroughly cleaned small intestine of sheep. These kinds of hot dogs are preferred by hot dog pushcarts because they maintain a much firmer texture and the snap that releases juices and flavor when this product is bitten into. Also, because of the natural casing, this will give your hot dogs a longer selling time.

Skinless hot dogs also must use a casing in the cooking process when the product is manufactured. The casing is usually a long tube of thin cellulose that is completely removed between cooking and packaging. Skinless hot dogs vary in the texture of the product surface but have a much softer bite than natural casing hot dogs. Skinless hot dogs are more uniform in shape and size than the natural casing hot dogs and are less expensive.

It would be wise to bring at least two hundred hot dogs with you to the site. A set delivery can be set up, or you can pick them up on an as-need basis. Sabrett natural casing #607 is recommended. If they are not available, you may substitute a similar product or contact a local wholesaler, and they might start to carry this product. They come in five-pound packages and, depending on size, have-twelve to a dozen. Since these are smoked, they will remain fresh as long as they are stored in a cool, dry, dark place. All unused hot dogs must be stored in a refrigerator upon closing for the day. Quality is most important. The price per pound is approximately $4.

Rolls

You should start with twenty dozen rolls. I recommend Sabrett hot dog rolls or a similar product. These hot dog rolls are specially made for the #607 natural-casing hot dog. Trademark secrets produce a texture that does not absorb the juices from the hot dog or condiments, preventing the hot dog roll from becoming waterlogged. They cost approximately $1.50 per dozen.

Ice

You will need ice for your cooler and fountain drinks if they are available. If you have freezer space available, buy ice in bulk. Retail ice sells for $1.50-$2.50 per bag. Wholesale or larger quantities might only run $1.00 per bag. If you plan to work five to seven days a week, you might want to invest in an ice machine.

Soda and Drinks

Soda is funny. Many name-brand sodas can be purchased at the supermarket or other outlets at a lower price than from suppliers. Keep your eye on the flyers; you can get some great deals. Keep the name brands simple.

- Coke or Pepsi
- Diet Coke or Diet Pepsi
- Sprite or Sierra Mist

You can experiment with others.

- Root beer
- Mountain Dew
- Ginger ale
- 7UP
- Orange and grape soda

Water is a must.

Drinks and Ades

Drinks and ades are very popular. Noff's can provide Citrus Heaven orange juice and lemonade. The cost is approximately $8.00 per jug. Each jug makes six gallons. Other specialty drinks and ades can be purchased depending on what your customer wants. You must add the cost of ice, cups, lids, and straws. Even with these additional costs, the profit can be enormous. These can also be sold at specialty events for $1.00-$1.50 per cup. If you work special events with custom cups, they can sell from $3.00 to $5.00 or higher with free refills. Private-label sodas are also available. This is very profitable and also offers name recognition. Check your local phone book or the Internet to see if any are in your area. Iced tea, Yoo-hoo, and power soft drinks are also very profitable.

Condiments

Condiments will come in two varieties. The first variety is generally cold and includes the following:

- Mustard
- Relish
- Ketchup
- Salt
- Red pepper
- Hot sauce
- Bacon bits
- Hot sauce
- Chopper onions

If you want to try something new, please be aware of spoilage. The second variety is hot, which includes the following:

Chili
Red onions
Sauerkraut
Cheddar cheese

These have to be hot and prepared beforehand. A proven recipe is provided for both the chili and red onions. The only exception is sauerkraut and cheddar cheese. These condiments can be purchased at low prices at either a supermarket or restaurant supply house. If there is anything that has a local appeal, be sure to offer that as well.

Note: Stand-alone carts and temporary trailers will have different requirement for condiments. If you are working a temporary location, premade packets might work better. Speed is more important than low cost. At a fixed location, quality and repeat customers are more important.

The most important thing when selling hot dogs is not to overload the condiments so they flow over the top of the bun. You might feel you are giving them something extra, but messy or sloppy hot dogs are hard to eat. Placing the requested condiments in the proper order and not overflowing the bun provides good-tasting and easy-to-eat hot dogs your customers will enjoy. As you become more experienced, you will know the proper proportions for each variation of hot dog ordered.

Potato Chips, Candy, etc.

You will need to offer something aside from just hot dogs. Chips, snacks, and candy are high-profit items and have a long shelf life. Twenty to thirty bags each of chips and candy should be fine to get started. Fresh fruits, homemade brownies or cookies, and packaged cakes are also something to consider. These are impulse items; hence, you want them to be in a visible location.

Water

Be sure to fill your water supply before setting out to your site. Five gallons is recommended, but if you need more, make sure you carry enough.

Napkins, Straws, Bags, Hot Dog Servers, Take-Out Containers, and Wipe Rags and Wet Wipes

Napkins, hot dog servers, and straws for drinks must be provided to your customers. Bags and take-out containers are for your customers who want to have their order to go. Wipe rags are needed to keep your cooking surface and hands clean.

Serving Utensils

You will need knives, forks, and spoons for serving purposes.

Cash Apron

It might be easier to work out of an apron than your pockets or a cash register. One of your largest challenges in operating a cart is collecting the money and making change. The more you can speed up this process, the better off you will be.

Credit Card and Debit Machine

The hot dog business is generally a cash business. But if you have the capability to accept credit or debit cards, you can increase sales. Please be advised that you have to pay a fee for these transactions, so you might want to set a minimum limit for these transactions.

Change

Be sure to bring at lease $87 in change. More is better:

Two ten-dollar bills
Five five-dollar bills
Twenty-five one-dollar bills
Ten dollars in quarters
Five dollars in dimes
Two dollars in nickels

More is better. There is nothing worse than losing a sale because you cannot make a change.

Garbage Containers

Even if there are enough trash containers in you area, always bring you own, or at least garbage bags, which you can tie to your cart or trailer. It is an absolute must to keep your area clean.

Extras

- Extra cooler
- Extra fuel supply
- Spare tire
- Lighters or matches

Keep Experimenting

If your have the capability to expand and offer other products, keep experimenting by trying out the following items:

- Coffee
- Hot sausages
- Hot pretzels
- Funnel cakes
- Pizza
- Churros
- Nachos
- Popcorn
- Cotton Candy
- Candy or caramel apples
- Peanuts
- Fresh-baked cookies or brownies
- Ice cream (seasonal)
- Italian ice (seasonal)

All of these items are very profitable and will keep your customers coming back.

At the Job Site

Everything you need to bring to the site might not be kept in the cart. This means you might need to use a trunk or a storage container. You would hate to run out of napkins, straws, or something essential and have to stop working just to run out and get them.

Your Work Area at Home

You should try to set aside an area in your home strictly for the operation of your cart. This is where you can store all of your stock. This is also a place where you can have a spare refrigerator or ice machine.

Do not store anything on the floor or on the ground. Always store foods on shelves raised above the floor or ground. These include foods that are prepackaged. Do not store any condiments or food near any cleaners or chemicals. These guidelines are designed to prevent them from becoming contaminated.

Also, you should have a dedicated area for you to do your paperwork and to properly file all of your financial information, business receipts, and important paperwork. You should have a computer located here. This can be for both business operation and marketing purposes.

Food Preparation

Note: Although we refer to cooking your hot dogs, in reality, hot dogs are already smoked when you purchase them. All you are really doing is heating them. Boiling is the preferred technique for cooking your hot dogs.

Boiling is Fast

Your goal in this business is to pump out volume. Boiling will allow you to make and sell the most hot dogs per hour. If you are in a high-volume situation, this will be the only way you will be able to keep hot dogs consistently available. People are also used to boiled hot dogs off a cart. Because the hot dog is already cooked, you can boil a hot dog in about sixty seconds. You will have to do some experimenting with this. Your goal is to serve the hot dog hot but not overcooked. If a hot dog is boiled too long, it will either split or get waterlogged and discolored. The key to an excellent boiled hot dog is when you bite into it, it has a snap. To keep its color, Noff's recommends you add white vinegar to your water.

Boiling is Efficient

Boiling is the most effective way to heat the entire hot dog.

No Lost Sales

The biggest advantage you have in this business is speed. McDonald's and Burger King are called fast food, but they cannot come close to competing with you in the speed at which you can deliver your product to the customer's hand. People today just do not want to wait for anything.

Boiling also allows the flavor of the hot dogs to seep into the water. This makes for a tastier hot dog (hence, dirty water dogs).

Remember This

In a recent survey, customers were asked their reason for purchasing food from a hot dog cart. This is not a scientific survey, but here are the answers:

Speed or convenience:	60 percent
I was hungry and I saw you:	25 percent
Other:	15 percent

In addition we found from the survey that 70 percent of the customers are regulars or had at least purchased from the same hot dog cart before. Hence repeat business is the key factor in you success.

Pricing

What you can charge for your hot dogs and drinks will depend on the area you are in. When pricing your items, try to keep the pricing simple. Noff's recommends $0.25 increments. This simplifies the math and requires you to only carry mostly quarters for change.

Note: You might want to offer value specials (sample provided below):

$5 for two hot dogs, one can of soda or bottled water, and one bag of chips
$6 for three hot dogs, one can of soda or bottled water, and chips

You decide. The key is to have them keep coming back, hopefully with coworkers, friends, and family. Remember, word of mouth is your best advertisement.

Condiment Handling

Your goal in dealing with your customer is to get their money and serve them a high-quality hot dog. Your method of condiment handling can vary depending on you location.

First, if you have a stand-only cart, you will want to handle the condiments yourself. You will be familiar with which condiment placements make for the best taste. Condiments should be applied in the following order. Any combination should still follow the same order, simply by subtracting the missing condiment:

1. Mustard
2. Ketchup
3. Cheese
4. Chopped Onions
5. Sauerkraut
6. Red onions
7. Chili
8. Relish

Pot set-up. Generally, if you have a three- or a four-pot setup, the hot condiments should be heated in this manner. Cook the hot dog in a half-sized, side-hinged pot directly over a burner. In this pot you can have chili, sauerkraut, or both. These condiments should be served hot. If you are serving onion sauce, the onions should be preheated or cooked prior to opening and served warm. If you are serving cheese, you do not have to preheat it; it is best served warm so as not to burn it. Depending on your volume, these condiments are served from smaller pots that are sunken into your hanging pots.

Note: Regional condiments will be determined on a case-by-case basis to better serve your customers.

Second, if you are dealing in extremely high volume or at temporary locations, you will find it much easier to limit your condiments. Also, to speed up the process, you can provide individual condiment packets.

Leftovers

After a successful day of selling, you will undoubtedly have leftovers. Since hot dogs are already cooked, they will be OK to serve another time. As long as all the unheated hot dogs are stored in a refrigerator or cooler, they will be OK to serve again next time you work. Depending on how long it will be, you might want to freeze them after closing up.

Perishable condiments have a short shelf life. Hot condiments, such as onions, chili, and cheese, can be used the following day. Please be advised you must refrigerate them immediately after closing for the day. I do not recommend saving sauerkraut. Since it is a very inexpensive condiment, you should not take any chances and start fresh every day. You must use your own judgment. I follow this rule: "*When in doubt, throw it out.*"

Cold condiments generally have a very long shelf life. They should be stored all in one box or container. Please be advised you must check them and make sure you have enough for the next time you work.

Dealing with People

You are going to develop regular customers. Some come for the food, and some will come just to bend your ear. Just remember this: the more you know about your customers, the better you will do. The longer they stay, the more they will buy. Also, it gives the appearance that your business is serving good food that people want. You are not there to spread gossip, but a little concern and a friendly face will go a long way.

If you are in a high-volume or temporary location, you might want to speed up this process. Long lines might turn off potential customers. Be businesslike. Do not encourage long conversations, but don't be too short either. Always keep in mind that your time is valuable and is best used by filling your pocket.

Keep Your Cart and Your Area Clean

Lack of cleanliness will be your biggest loser of business. People will likely not be impressed if your cart and area are clean, but they will not be unimpressed if your area is not spotless. You should clean your cooking and serving area all the time. You should clean your area before you leave for the day and clean your cart thoroughly when you close. Since most of the parts and the cart are stainless steel, this is not a difficult task.

Maintaining Your Equipment

Check to make sure your hot dog cart in running properly. Check all the appliances and the stove to verify if it is working and that you have enough fuel supply. Check your tires and lights on both your hot dog cart and pulling vehicle. Note overall appearance and make a list of any items missing or what needs to be repaired.

Safety Guidelines

- *Thunderstorms and lightning.* Hot dog carts are generally designed to work year-round and in all kinds of weather, but lightning is the exception. If you see a lightning storm approaching, you should close down and seek proper shelter.
- *Fire.* Fires rarely happen. No matter what the requirement, I suggest you have a properly functioning fire extinguisher.
- *First aid.* Always keep a first-aid kit in your cart or storage area to treat small burns, nicks, cuts, and abrasions that will occur.
- *Sun safety.* Try to park in the shade. Prolonged sun exposure and sunburn are constant health hazards because you are located out of doors at the peek sun periods of the day. Wear a hat that completely covers your head, try to position in the shade or under an umbrella, wear sunblock, and drink plenty of fluids.
- *Towing a trailer.* Always check your hot dog cart's trailer hitch and make sure it is pushed down and locked. Make sure you have the right ball for your hitch and you connect safety chains. Connect the electrical wires and make sure all your tires are inflated. Finally make sure everything is tied down and secure.

Growing Your Hot Dog Empire

The fastest and easiest way to grow sales is to add strategic items. These do not have to be just food items.

On St Patrick's Day, add green hats, buttons, and anything green. On the Fourth of July, you can have a variety of patriotic items available. You can also carry local souvenirs.

Find ways to advertise for free. Hand out flyers with your name, hours of operation, address, and any specials. Use free materials from vendors. For example, if you are selling Sabbret hot dogs, you can obtain an umbrella or stickers, Coke and Pepsi signs, etc. These logs and brand colors on your cart's signage draw attention.

Put on a show. Having a hot dog cart or trailer is not the same thing as going to a gourmet restaurant, but it is still a service business. You are on stage when you are running a stand. A good personality brings people back. The clanging sound of stainless steel pots gets people's attention. Have fun while you are doing these activities, and people will notice. Try to have happy and positive background sounds. Have happy music or a good ball game on. This keeps your customers happy and might make them stay a little longer, resulting in goodwill and more sales.

Another way to grow faster is to operate more carts. By getting to the point of operating your first cart, you have overcome most obstacles. Why let this experience go to waste? Future carts will be easy to get going.

Finally, the best way is word of mouth. Making a good-tasting, reasonably priced hot dog will make people come back and recommend you to others.

BUSINESS BASICS

Appearance

A person's overall appearance must be neat and convey the attitude of professionalism. Clothing should be clean and without stains. A fresh change of clothing should be worn each day. Clothing should not be frayed or worn out. Proper shorts can be worn. No bikinis or halters should be worn. We have all heard of women selling hot dogs in bikinis, but I am promoting more professional attire. Males should be clean shaven and have neat hair.

Food and Health Hygiene

Poor personal hygiene, especially lack of proper hand washing, is unacceptable. The following are typical health-code guidelines:

1. Finger nails must be clipped.
2. Long hair must be tied back, pinned, or in a net.
3. Hands must be washed after using the toilet, coughing, sneezing, blowing your nose, or handling garbage or any other unsanitary item.
4. No smoking or tobacco chewing.
5. No chewing gum.
6. Do not eat or drink when serving food.
7. Do not work when you are sick.
8. Clothing must be clean.
9. Cross contamination is not allowed between raw and cooked foods.

Advertising and Promotions

The first step is creating a complete marketing package. Look at each element of your operation. Everything from parking, the design of your printed materials, and the design of your equipment should be an accurate reflection of your business operation.

Introduce yourself to your area. Print up some flyers offering coupons and take them to local businesses. Tape them to mailboxes. Post them in supermarkets and any other place where you can put them. The flyers should include your location, hours of operation, specials, and contact information if available.

You can also have a professional Web site designed. Most simple Web sites are not expensive to create. A simple one should have a photo of your operation, your address, and your hours of operation. If you have editing capabilities, you can offer food specials or coupons and add customers to an e-mail distribution list.

You should have professional signage. If you have the ability, put up sandwich boards or other signs two hundred to three hundred yards down the roads to pull in traffic. Images from your suppliers and a bright umbrella are very eye-catching.

You can attempt to promote yourself in local papers. Some have special sections dedicated to local business and what they feature. A good news article can do wonders. You might also experiment with paid advertising. After a while, you will know what works keep the winners and discard the losers.

Selling

Successful selling involves more than just putting up a sign and waiting for customers to come to you. It is a selling cycle: attracting customers, encouraging sales, and satisfying their needs. This will insure the continuing growth and success of your business. Remember this rule: it is easier to keep a current happy customer than to attract a new one.

Once you have attracted your customer, you have to close the sale. You must have a clear idea of your product. Professional signs will make this process simple for your customer. You must be able to service your customer even if you get many customers at once. You must ask for the sale.

Always try to up-sell. It is very simple. Just ask a positive question with a positive suggestion. Do not ask "Would you like a drink with that?" Ask "What kind of drink would you like with that?" If a customer is indecisive or unsure, help them. Say, "Would you like to try chili or onions?"

Customers will not see this as up-selling, but rather as you showing a personal interest in them.

There are no hard-and-fast rules on pricing. You will have to price your hot dogs and other products based on your market. I advise to keep the prices in twenty-five-cent increments. This will make your math simple, and it will be easier to make change. This will speed up your transaction time. You might also want to have price specials. Once your customers know them, they will eventually pay with exact change.

How you speak to your customer is very important. Always be friendly and upbeat. A smile and a simple hello can go a long way. After a while, you will start to know your customers' names and be familiar with their orders as you see them approach. And always make sure you keep everything neat and clean.

Customer Database and Follow-up

Embrace technology. Nothing is worse than having a satisfied customer and then not following up and asking for more sales. Whether you are working a permanent or temporary location, you must make a list and keep in touch with your customers.

Permanent customers will require more contact to keep them updated on special offers and any new products you add. Learn how to use the computer or hire a marketing person. Have your customers fill out a forms with their name, address, e-mail, and, if a business, their fax number. A simple postcard or e-mail sent to your customers can generate a lot of repeat business from happy customers. There are also several marketing companies who send out e-mails and faxes on a daily basis to your contacts. You might be surprised by how affordable these services can be.

Temporary locations require a different type of follow-up. Keep a list of all the functions you work. If you worked a promotional event for a business, give them a call or send them a thank-you letter asking if your services are needed again. Sometimes out of sight is out of mind. They might have lost your contact information and do not know how to contact you. A postcard, call, or e-mail every three months should keep you and your service fresh in their minds.

If you work events, please keep a list of when they are. Nothing is worse than forgetting about an event you made a lot of money at. Set your calendar in advance. This way you will know what events are coming up and plan your schedule accordingly. With today's computers, you can set up a reminder years in advance. If you cannot use a computer, you can always use a Rolodex.

Simple Bookkeeping

Unless you are very familiar with accounting and tax Preparation, a simple, straightforward bookkeeping system is important. Good bookkeeping will enable you to analyze your business on an ongoing basis.

For most people, I advise you to keep it simple. The only real skills you will need are the ability to count, record, add, and subtract. Forms can be obtained at an office supply store or found on the Internet.

You will need to keep all of you receipts in order to keep accurate records, both for your own information and to show the government agencies at tax time. Never rely on your memory. Put it in writing. Keeping your records simple and up-to-date will also save you time and money when you actually need an accountant at tax time.

Make a file or folder that can hold all of your business-related expenses, including day-to-day supplies, equipment expenses, pay, office supplies, loan interest, and vehicle mileage or fuel. Keep business items separate from personal expense items. If they are on the same receipt, please highlight it.

Keep your records in a safe place. Make a separate folder or file for each of the different types of expenses, such as food, equipment purchases, repair and service receipts, advertising, office supplies, business expenses, and any other category that might be required for your business.

Sample Commissary Letter

Date

To whom it may concern:

Please be advised I am allowing *you or your business's name* to use my facility for all inspection needed to operate their business. This will not be limited to receiving and storing any inventory, cooking food, cleaning all equipment, and disposal of any waste.

If you have any questions, please do not hesitate to contact me.

Thank you,

Owner's/Manager's Name

My advice is to keep it as simple as possible. You might also need a copy of their current health inspection license.

Noff's Onion Recipe

Ingredients:

10 pounds Spanish or yellow onions
1 teaspoon garlic powder
1 teaspoon black pepper
1 6-ounce can tomato paste
¼ cup oil (corn, vegetable, or canola)
2 cups water
1 tablespoon salt

In a large container of warm water add salt, garlic powder, black pepper, tomato paste, and oil. Cut the onions into slivers by pealing the onion, cutting it in half, and then cutting it into slivers.

Simmer mixture at a low boil for 1 to 1 1/2 hours or until onions are soft with no crunch. Note that yellow onions might require a slightly longer cooking time.

Noff's Hot Dog Chili

Ingredients:

5 pounds 80 percent lean chopped meat
1 8-ounce can tomato sauce
1 teaspoon garlic powder
1 teaspoon black pepper
11 teaspoons chili powder
2 teaspoons cayenne powder
2 teaspoons sugar
2 tablespoons salt
1 cup water

In a large pot of warm water, add the salt. Then mix the chopped meat, breaking it up into a slurry mix. Then add the tomato sauce, garlic powder, black pepper, chili powder, cayenne powder, and sugar.

Slowly simmer for 1 1/2 to 2 hours until fully cooked. Be sure to stir the mixture every 5 to 10 minutes to keep it loose.

Note: If you want to thicken it up, add bread crumbs halfway through the cooking process.

Hot Dog Specials

2 all-beef Sabrett hot dogs
1 can of soda or water
1 bag of chips

$5
*All toppings included

3 all-beef Sabrett hot dogs
1 can of soda or water
1 bag of chips

$6
*All toppings included

Address:
Hours of operation:
Contact information:

A Unique Form of Advertising Party Fun

Give away *free* hot dogs to promote your business or event. You will have a full-size hot dog cart or trailer manned by a professional hot dog vendor.

Cost

Three-hour rental:	$300
Four-hour rental:	$350
Five-hour rental:	$375

Food Package

120 hot dogs and rolls:	$100
180 hot dogs and rolls:	$140
240 hot dogs and rolls:	$180
Call for larger amounts	

All hot dogs will be high-quality, pushcart-style hot dogs and come with mustard and ketchup. Sauerkraut and cheddar cheese can be provided for an additional charge of $25. Napkins and hot dog holders will be provided.

Contact information:

Follow the Manual Guidelines and Suggestions

Become familiar with the contents of this manual. This information has been carefully designed from over ninety years of family experience. It will save you time, money, and frustration.

The manual will help you through daily operations and will keep you, your hot dog cart, and your customers happy and healthy.

Once you decide what type of business you want to operate, simply follow these instructions step-by-step and soon you will be on your way to running you very own hot dog business.

Notes:

INDEX

Q

quality, 22-23, 29, 52, 64

R

red onions, 47
Registration expenses, 31-32
relish, 9, 15, 36, 46, 52
Rolodex, 58

S

Sabrett, 45, 63
salt, 17, 46, 61-62
sauerkraut, 15, 17, 36, 47, 52-53, 64
seasonal changes, 40
Seasonings, 17
selling, 24, 29, 37, 41, 44, 47, 53-54, 56-57
Selling Strategy, 24
7-Eleven, 23
"Sic Wove Overcoats, The," 18
Sierra Mist, 45
skinless hot dogs, 44
soda, 18, 36, 41, 45, 51, 63
sole proprietorship, 19
Sonic Drive-In, 23
Sprite, 45
Start-up Costs, 39
Storage, 31, 33, 39, 50, 54
St. Patrick's Day, 41
strength-in-numbers principle, 29

T

technology, 58

V

vegetarian hot dogs, 15
vending cart, 27
vendors, 17-18, 22, 24, 28-30, 37, 54, 64
Von de Ahe, Chris, 17

W

water, 18, 28, 34, 36, 46-47, 51, 61-63
Web site, 57
Wienerschnitzel, 23
Woody's Chicago Style, 23

Y

Yale Record, The, 18
Yoo-hoo, 36, 46

Z

Zoning requirements, 31-32